CHANUTE PUBLIC LIBRARY
111 North Lincoln
CHANUTE, KS 66720

FOOD
AROUND THE WORLD

BY
PATRICIA LAKIN

BLACKBIRCH PRESS, INC.
WOODBRIDGE, CONNECTICUT

CONTENTS

Published by Blackbirch Press, Inc.
260 Amity Road
Woodbridge, CT 06525
e-mail: staff@blackbirch.com
website: www.blackbirch.com

©1999 Blackbirch Press, Inc.
First Edition

All rights reserved. No part of this book may be reproduced in any form without permission in writing from Blackbirch Press, Inc., except by a reviewer.

Printed in Singapore

10 9 8 7 6 5 4 3 2 1

Photo Credits
Cover, pp. 3, 5, 7, 9 (bottom), 15 (top), 17, 19 (bottom), 25 (both), 29: ©Corel Corporation; pp. 1, 9 (top), 11, 15 (bottom), 19 (top), 29 (inset): ©PhotoDisc; p. 13: ©O. Louis Mazzatenta/National Geographic; p. 21 (both): Air India; p. 23: ©Alwan Interactive; p. 27: ©Stockman; p. 31: Tom and Michelle Grimm/International Stock Photo.

Library of Congress Cataloging–in–Publication Data
Lakin, Patricia.
   Food around the world / by Patricia Lakin.
     p. cm.—(We all share)
   Includes bibliographical references and index.
   Summary: Looks at different kinds of food and drink and related customs around the world, including tea in Russia, hot dogs in the United States, and baklava in Greece.
     ISBN 1-56711-147-5
      1.Games—Cross-cultural studies—
        Juvenile literature. I. Title. II. Series.
TX355.L14   1999
641.3—dc20   98-50549
                                      CIP
                                      AC

INTRODUCTION	3
RUSSIA	4
UNITED STATES	6
MEXICO	8
ENGLAND	10
COLOMBIA	12
NATIVE AMERICAN	14
GREECE	16
CHINA	18
INDIA	20
IRAQ	22
SAUDIA ARABIA	24
ETHIOPIA	26
CANADA	28
ISRAEL	30
GLOSSARY	32
FOR MORE INFORMATION	32
INDEX	32

INTRODUCTION

In 1492, Christopher Columbus set sail from Spain to find a shorter route to the West Indies. He was searching for gold, but also for spices. More than 200 years before Columbus set out, Marco Polo left Italy and traveled to the Far East, reaching China. He returned with new foods and spices from the different areas he visited.

The food of a country is always a special part of the culture and identity of that country. People tend to create dishes from the foods and spices that grow in their area. But, long ago, traders, invaders, and explorers exposed people of one country to the foods and spices of another. If the people of a country developed a taste for a foreign food or spice, they tried to grow it. If they couldn't, they traded some of their goods for it. There is no country in the world today that has not had its foods and seasonings influenced by the traders and invaders of long ago.

Spices have been bought and traded for hundreds of years.

RUSSIA

Russia's long, cold winters limit the fruits and vegetables that can grow.

Russia is a huge country. Each region experiences very different climates, many of which are harsh. Long, cold winters limit the amount of fruits and vegetables that can grow year round.

Because meat is scarce and expensive, Russians base their diet on breads, sour cream, potatoes, cabbage, and beets. Fish is available more often than meat is. Caviar—the eggs from a sturgeon fish—is a favorite of Russians who can afford it. Most caviar is an expensive luxury food.

A Russian may fight off the early morning cold by having a bowl of warm beet soup, called borscht.

Lunch is usually the big meal of the day. It could feature a fish soup called rassolinik. Pirozhkis—stuffed dumplings—are another popular food.

A lighter dinner may consist of eating lunch-time leftovers, or cabbage-stuffed pancakes called blinis. Blinis are often topped with sour cream.

Tea is the most popular hot drink. It is served with each meal from the family's prized teapot, or samovar.

Right: The world's best caviar comes from Russia, though it is too expensive for most Russians to buy.
Below: Farmers sell potatoes at an open-air Russian market. Potatoes and other root vegetables form a large part of the Russian diet.

UNITED STATES

The most popular foods in the United States reflect a broad variety of cultures and ingredients.

The United States of America is a vast land that grows a wide variety of foods. It also has a wide variety of cultures. The most popular restaurant chains reflect those cultures. They serve everything from Italian pizzas to Mexican tacos to Chinese egg rolls to the popular relative of the German sausage that Americans call hot dogs. Salsa and guacamole—Mexican-born "sauces"—are top sellers in U.S. supermarkets. American-born foods are also part of the restaurant scene. They include Southern fried chicken, barbecued ribs, or "Philly" cheese steaks. American dessert favorites include chocolate cake, apple pie, ice cream, or donuts.

Perhaps the best-known American foods are found not at a restaurant, but in a stadium where the most American of games is played—baseball.

At a baseball game, vendors can be heard calling out the names of some of America's most popular foods: popcorn, cotton candy, hot dogs, hamburgers, and soda!

The average American family eats three meals a day, and dinner is the main meal. Traditionally, meat or chicken is served along with a starch dish (rice, potato, pasta) and vegetable.

Among "American" foods, perhaps the best-known are hot dogs, hamburgers, and apple pie.

MEXICO

The ancient people of Mexico were the first to grow and prepare many of the foods we know today.

Almost 9,000 years ago, the ancient people of Mexico grew corn, tomatoes, and avocados. They also served turkey, duck, and shellfish. And, they were the first people to grow cacao beans and make chocolate!

These foods are found around the world today, and are still part of many of Mexico's most popular dishes.

Tomatoes are plentiful in Mexico. They are used in many native dishes, including the spicy tomato sauce called salsa. Avocados are also used in main dishes, as well as in the avocado-and-onion "sauce" or dip called guacamole. These dishes, as well as many others, often include various chilies, which are very spicy peppers.

Corn is still a major crop in Mexico, and it is used in many forms. It is the main ingredient in the thin Mexican flour pancake, or tortilla. Coarsely ground corn is used to make another Mexican dish, the tamale. Tamales are big dumplings stuffed with meat or vegetables, and then steamed in corn husks.

Right: A traditional clay pot filled with cooked beans sits with a basket of tortillas and a bowl of red salsa.
Below: Spicy, hot chili peppers—being sold in this Mexican market (center) are used in many traditional Mexican dishes.

ENGLAND

England's fertile farm country provides a wealth of dairy products, meat, and vegetables.

This island country has a large area of fertile farm land. Vegetables and dairy products are plentiful. But England is known mostly for its favorite beverage—tea. Serving late afternoon tea with a snack has been an English tradition for almost 400 years.

Tea was, and still is, grown primarily in India and China. In the 1600s, English traders brought tea back to England, and the drink has never lost its popularity. Throughout England, between 4 and 5 p.m. children and adults will stop their activities for tea time. With their tea, the English may snack on small sandwiches. Jam and scones—similar to fluffy biscuits—are another favorite.

Because of this late afternoon mini-meal, the English have supper around 7 p.m. A typical English dinner is shepherd's pie, which is a chopped meat stew mixed with vegetables, topped with mashed potatoes. The dish is baked in the oven and served piping hot.

If the family eats out, they may order fish and chips (French fries) at the local pub. A pub is both a bar and restaurant. In England, especially in smaller towns, the pub serves as a gathering place where friends and families get together. They not only eat there, but also chat, sing, play darts, and watch soccer matches on television.

Fish and chips, traditionally served in newspaper, is an English pub "classic." The chips are often eaten with vinegar instead of ketchup.

COLOMBIA

This South American country is high in the Andes Mountains, where only certain kinds of fruits and vegetables can grow.

Colombia is the fourth-largest country in South America. It is home to the northernmost part of the Andes Mountains.

Centuries ago, in those same mountain slopes, the native people cultivated the potato. They even developed a simple way to freeze-dry this root vegetable. They sliced the potato and left it so that it would freeze during the cold mountain nights. Once the sliced potato dried out, it could be stored for long periods of time without spoiling. And, it could be instantly ground to make flour.

These Colombians are enjoying a feast that includes a variety of grilled meats, corn, and many root vegetables.

Throughout South America today, the potato—along with many other vegetables—is still an important food. Colombia's capital city, Bogotá, prizes their famous dish, ajiaco de pollo. This is a chicken stew that also includes potatoes, maize (corn), cabbage, and manioc—a plant with edible starchy roots. This stew is served with cream, capers, and bits of avocado.

For dessert, Colombians almost always choose fruit. Many fruits sold in the United States and Europe grow in Colombia. But, many unusual fruits such as maracuya, lulo, pitahaya, and curuba, can only be enjoyed in Colombia.

NATIVE AMERICAN

Native Americans taught English settlers a great deal about growing and preparing foods in North America.

The Wampanoag were the first Native Americans to welcome the English settlers who landed at Plymouth, Massachusetts in 1620.

These Native Americans taught the English many things about farming and surviving in North America. They also introduced the settlers to the popular Native American food—corn.

The Wampanoags also found plentiful shellfish in the waters off New England. Shellfish and roasted corn are the two main ingredients in the Wampanoag's famous meal, the clambake.

The clambake is more than just a meal, it is a beach picnic. Lobsters, clams, and corn make up the feast, which takes a great deal of time and effort to prepare. First, a big pit is dug in the sand. Rocks are heated and placed in the hole. Seaweed is carried from the ocean and placed in the pit with the rocks. The lobsters and clams are cooked as they are added to the red-hot rocks and seaweed. Corn, still in its husk, is also placed in the huge hot pile.

The classic clambake includes corn and various kinds of shellfish, including lobster, clams, and mussels.

GREECE

The dry, rocky soil of Greece makes it hard to grow a wide variety of fruits and vegetables. Olive trees and seafood are plentiful.

Much of Greece and its islands are dotted with rocky hills, making the land difficult to plow. As a result, a limited variety of foods are grown there. But tomatoes, eggplants, and olives grow plentifully. Livestock, such as goats and sheep, thrive on Greece's many hillsides.

Since people in Greece are never more than 85 miles away from the sea, fish is another important food. This is why fish, goat, and lamb products are the key ingredients in popular Greek dishes.

Along with a flat bread called pita, Greeks often start the day with a breakfast of feta (goat cheese), olives, and tomatoes. The noon lunch is the heaviest meal of the day. It may feature moussaka, which is a vegetable, lamb, and cheese dish. Another possible favorite is souvlaki, which is barbecued lamb on a skewer.

Baklava is a popular dessert. The sticky, sweet, many-layered pastry is made with a very flaky dough, shaped in a triangle and stuffed with honey and nut filling.

Typical Greek dishes feature fresh, simply grilled meats or seafood and simple salads that use a lot of olive oil.

CHINA

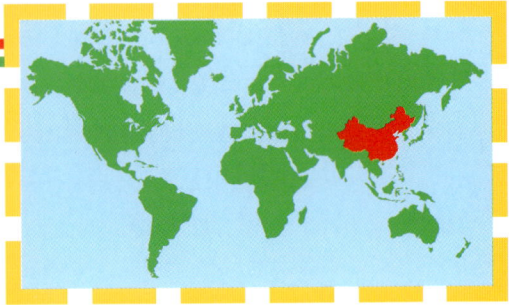

For the people of China, food is thought to be an important part of physical and mental health.

China is the world's third-largest country. It is divided into many regions including Szechwan, Peking, Shanghai, and Canton. Each region has its own unique style of cooking. But no matter what the cooking style, food is more than just something to eat for the Chinese. In China, food is linked to both physical and mental health. This philosophy is taught in an ancient Chinese religion, Taoism. Taoism speaks of the importance of living off the land. That is one of the main reasons that Chinese dishes consist mainly of vegetables. And the ingredients in all Chinese dishes have to be absolutely fresh.

Rice is harvested in the southern parts of China. It is the main staple in the Chinese diet. Noodles, however, are the staple of the diet in northern China. There, the climate is very harsh, and rice cannot be grown in such great amounts.

Throughout China, people seem to follow the same rituals for eating their meals. The family gathers at a round table. Dinner usually starts with a soup, one rice or noodle dish, and then four meat, vegetable, or fish dishes. Each member of the family gets a small bowl of rice. Everyone uses two wooden sticks, called chopsticks, to pick up and eat their food.

Above: Chinese food is often cooked quickly in a bowl-like skillet, called a wok.
Below: Outdoor restaurants, like all restaurants in China, feature fresh ingredients that are cooked to order and served right away.

INDIA

Most people in India are Hindu. In the Hindu religion, beef is not allowed to be eaten because cows are considered sacred.

India is known as the home of many herbs and spices. Tamarind, tumeric, saffron, gingeroot, cumin, cinnamon, cardamom, and cilantro are just a few of the best-known flavorings.

India is also a country with many kinds of bread. Dishes may be served with big, round, flat crisp wafers called poppadums, or round, flat wheat bread called roti. Nan is roti bread that has been cooked in a clay oven called a tandoor. There is also chapati, which is a flat, unleavened bread that is cooked on a griddle and then toasted on charcoal. Chapati, like many of the Indian breads, can be eaten by itself or as a scoop for other dishes. For many traditional

Indian dishes, knives and forks are not used. Instead, the bread serves as a utensil.

Religion affects how and what an Indian may eat. For Hindus, the cow is a sacred animal. Therefore, Hindis never eat beef. Muslims are forbidden to eat pork. Chicken, fish, goat, rice, and vegetables can be eaten by Indians of either religion and are common in many dishes.

Traditionally, Indians eat their meals with their right hand. (The left hand is considered unclean.) All the courses of a meal, including dessert, may be served at the same time. All of the plates are put in front of each diner on a round metal tray called a thali.

Top right: Ground, spiced meats and vegetables are common ingredients in many Indian dishes.
Right: An Indian vegetable stall features a wide variety of fresh ingredients.

Iraq is a Middle Eastern Muslim country, where the religion of Islam forbids pork to be eaten.

Traditional Iraqi food is similar to that of other Middle Eastern countries. As with its neighbors, there are ancient traditions surrounding Iraqi foods, how they are eaten, and how they are served.

Traditionally, Iraqis have farmed the land to produce wheat, eggplant, okra, olives, zucchini, nuts, figs, and dates. Iraqis raise sheep and goats, and use the goat's milk to make cheese and yogurt.

Pork is not served in Iraq because it is forbidden by the Muslim religion.

A typical breakfast may consist of bread, fruit, yogurt, nuts, and honey. Iraqi coffee, made from mocha beans, is thick and sweet. It is drunk throughout the day. Lunch is a small meal and may include a chick-pea spread called hummus. The hummus is scooped up in pita bread. The evening meal is generally the largest meal of the day. In most Iraqi households, before anyone eats, soapy water is passed around in a jug so the diners can wash their hands. First, the men eat. When they are done, the women eat. The food is served in one dish and people eat with their fingers. The polite way is to use only one's thumb and first two fingers.

A creamy spread made from chick peas and spices, called hummus (large bowl), is a popular food and a standard ingredient in many Iraqi dishes. A smoky spread or dip, called babaganoush (small bowl), is made from eggplant and spices.

SAUDI ARABIA

Because Saudi Arabia is mostly desert, very little can be grown or raised on its land.

Saudi Arabia is mostly a desert country. Only a very small part of the land can be used to grow crops or raise animals. Most of the food eaten here has to be imported.

In the remote villages of Saudi Arabia, where daily life follows the ancient ways, people sit on the floor with their legs crossed and eat with their hands.

Like their Middle Eastern neighbors, Saudis throughout the country also eat a round, flat bread with their meals. Their bread, called arikah, is often

A group of Saudi men enjoy a large meal together.
Right: Shish kebab can include a wide variety of vegetables and meats.

torn off and held in a spoon-like shape. This way, it can scoop up the side dish of honey that is often served with meals.

Saudis eat dairy foods, nuts, vegetables, grains, and fruits. Because Saudi Arabia is a Muslim country, pork is forbidden. Chicken and lamb, however, are very popular. A traditional Saudi meal, shish kebab, is a charcoal-cooked lamb dish that is served on a bed of rice.

Tea or coffee is served with all meals. People also like to drink camel's milk or the thicker laban, which is a yogurt drink.

ETHIOPIA

Ethiopia's climate can be harsh. Because little rain falls there, food shortages are common.

Ethiopia is on the east coast of Africa. It is close to the equator and has a hot climate all year long. Rainfall here can be very high or very low. There have been times when Ethiopia has had severe draughts (long periods with no rain). Without rain, crops cannot grow and food shortages follow. Because of this harsh climate, there is a flexibility in many Ethiopian dishes. If one ingredient is scarce, another can be used in its place. And, like many other African countries, Ethiopian recipes are not always written down. Rather, they are verbally passed on from one generation to the next.

Open-air markets in Ethiopia sell spices and vegetables, but a harsh climate often makes food scarce.

In Ethiopia's capital city, Addis Ababa, Ethiopians prepare foods in more modern ways. Stoves and microwave ovens are used, and Western cultures have influenced the types of foods that are eaten. But in the small villages, meals are made the way they have been for centuries. Women traditionally prepare the food, often cooking over an open fire. Generally, two meals are eaten each day, at noon and in the evening. Both may be a thick stew or soup, accompanied by Ethiopian bread called ingera. This is a flat, sour kind of bread.

CANADA

Canada is a huge country, rich in natural resources. Forests, oceans, lakes, and vast prairies provide a great variety of foods.

Canada is the second-largest country in the world. Much of its population has come from other lands. As a result, one can find authentic food from China, Russia, Germany, and France, along with a variety of foods from other cultures.

Canada is home to rich forest land and well-stocked lakes, rivers, and streams. It also has an ocean on both its eastern and western borders. Because of these natural resources, there are two foods often associated with the country—salmon and maple syrup. Salmon is found in many of Canada's lakes and streams. When its many sugar maple trees are tapped (drained) every March, they give forth their sticky sap. The sap is boiled down for hours to produce maple syrup. This syrup is commonly used as a topping for another food often linked with Canada—pancakes. Canadian pancakes are often served with Canadian bacon, which are salty slices of ham-like meat.

Canadians have found many ways to use and eat maple syrup. Below is maple "tire"— maple syrup that is boiled down and poured over snow to create a chewy "candy."
Inset: Pancakes and maple syrup.

ISRAEL

Most Israelis are Jewish, which means they are forbidden by their religion to eat pork or shellfish.

Israel is a relatively new country with an ancient past. For centuries, Arabs and Jews have lived in this Middle Eastern country side by side. When Israel was declared a Jewish state in 1948, many more Jews from other lands settled in their new homeland. The Russian, Moroccan, and Eastern European Jews, along with Jews from America, brought with them recipes for their favorite foods. But many typical Middle Eastern dishes are still commonly eaten in Israel as well.

Much of Israel is desert, so people in this country have had to work hard to grow fruits and vegetables here. Since 1948, farms have become very successful at cultivating a wide variety of citrus fruits and many other foods.

Israelis eat mostly fruits, vegetables, and dairy foods. Pork is not kosher—it is a forbidden food according to the Jewish religion (as well as for Muslims). It is not commonly found in Israel. Other meats are scarce, but turkey, chicken, and fish—especially St. Peter's fish—are eaten frequently. Shellfish, also not kosher, is rarely seen.

Tomatoes grow well here, and are often served at breakfast with cucumbers. Figs, watermelon, pita bread, and coffee typically accompany the breakfast meal.

Dinner may consist of a salad, or of dairy foods. Felafel in pita "pocket" bread may also be offered. Felafel is made from ground-up and spiced chick peas. The mixture is rolled into ball shapes, deep fried, and served with lettuce, tomatoes, and a creamy sauce.

Many fruits have been cultivated in Israel and now grow plentifully. Right, a vendor proudly displays his fresh strawberries.

GLOSSARY

authentic the real thing.

cultivate grow and harvest something.

delicacy a rare and often expensive specialty food.

draught a period of dry weather where there is little or no rain.

fertile land that is rich in nutrients.

immigrant a person who moves from the country of his or her birth to live in a new country.

philosophy a set of ideas about a given subject.

ritual certain actions or ceremonies that are done in the same way on a regular basis.

rural far from a city.

unleavened non-rising; this kind of bread is made with no yeast and does not rise.

vendors people who sell items, often from carts or trays.

FOR MORE INFORMATION

Books

Bruckhardt, Ann L. *Mexican Food & Culture* (Multicultural Cookbook Series). Danbury, CT: Children's Press, 1998.

Burns, Diane. Cheryl Walsh Bellville (Photographer). *Sugaring Season: Making Maple Syrup* (Photo Books). Minneapolis, MN: Carolrhoda Books, 1990.

Denny, Roz. *A Taste of China*. Chatham, NJ: Raintree/Steck Vaughn, 1997.

Miller, Jay. *American Indian Foods* (True Books). Danbury, CT: Children's Press, 1996.

Web Site

The Food Museum

Features descriptions of many foods—www.foodmuseum.com/~hughes/first.htm.

INDEX

Ajiaco de pollo, 13
Apple pie, 7
Arikah, 24
Avocado, 8, 13
Baklava, 17
Blinis, 5
Borscht, 4
Cacao, 8
Canadian bacon, 29
Caviar, 4
Chapati, 20
Chicken, 21, 25, 31
Chips, 11
Coffee, 7, 22, 25
Corn, 8, 14
Felafel, 31
Feta, 17
Fish, 4, 31
Fruit, 13, 22, 31
Goat, 16, 21
Guacamole, 6, 9
Hamburger, 7
Hindu, 20–21
Honey, 22, 25
Hot dogs, 6, 7
Hummus, 23
Ingera, 27
Kosher, 31
Laban, 25
Lamb, 16, 25
Maize, 13
Maple syrup, 28–29
Maple "tire," 29
Moussaka, 17
Muslim, 21, 22, 25, 31
Nan, 20
Noodles, 19
Pancakes, 29
Pirozhkis, 5
Pita bread, 17
Poppadums, 20
Potatoes, 4–5, 12, 13
Rassolinik, 5
Rice, 19, 21
Roti, 20
Salmon, 28
Salsa, 8
Scones, 11
Shellfish, 8, 15
Shepherd's pie, 11
Shish kebab, 25
Souvlaki, 17
Spices, 20
St. Peter's fish, 31
Tamales, 9
Taoism, 18
Tea, 5, 10, 11
Tortilla, 9
Wok, 19